Round the corner,
not far away...

Bing is sharing a book with

_____ today!

(you!)

HarperCollins *Children's Books*

ACAMARFILMS

Copyright © 2016 Acamar Films Ltd

First published in the UK in 2016 by HarperCollins Children's Books, a division of HarperCollins Publishers Ltd, 1 London Bridge Street, London, SE1 9GF

10 9 8 7 6 5 4 3 2 1

ISBN: 978-0-00-812238-6

The Bing television series is an Acamar Films production, co-produced in association with Brown Bag Films and adapted from the original books by Ted Dewan

Written by Mandy Archer

Edited by Stella Gurney, Freddie Hutchins and An Vrombaut

Designed by Anna Lubecka, Gary Knight and Pei Yi Tong

MIX
Paper from
responsible sources
FSC C007454

www.fsc.org

FSC™ is a non-profit international organisation established to promote the responsible management of the world's forests. Products carrying the FSC label are independently certified to assure consumers that they come from forests that are managed to meet the social, economic and ecological needs of present and future generations, and other controlled sources.

Find out more about HarperCollins and the environment at
www.harpercollins.co.uk/green

Bing™ Annual 2017

All about Bing... and all about me

This is **Bing.**

Bing has **black** hair and **green** eyes.

Bing is a **boy** bunny.

Here's Bing when he was a **baby.** He looks **very** little.

This is **me!**

I have .... hair

and .... eyes.

I am ⬭ a boy.

⬭ a girl.

When I was a baby, I looked like **this**

Bing is growing **taller** all the time

...and **SO** am I!

On .... ,
(date)
I was .... high.

On .... ,
(date)
I was .... high.

On .... ,
(date)
I was .... high.

Bing can feel:

happy

smiley

giggly

sad

upset

scared

quiet

busy

noisy

silly

bouncy

How am I feeling?

....

Bing has a **knack** – a special
thing that only **he** can do.
Bing can make his ears go:

pick

pock!

Sula can do
trumpet-blowing:

toot
toot!

My special knack is

....

....

7

This is **Bing's** house...

and this is his **bedroom.**

Bing's bedroom has **blue** walls and **yellow** curtains.

This is **my** house...

and this is where I sleep every night!

My bedroom has ....walls

and .... curtains.

Flop looks after Bing. Whenever Bing needs him, Flop knows just what to do. Bing loves Flop very much.

The people who look after me are

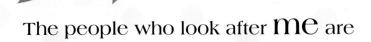

I love them very much, too.

In my family, there are

.... people.

Bing doesn't have any brothers or sisters, but he does have two cousins – Coco and Charlie. Coco is older than Bing and Charlie is still a baby.

Sometimes when Bing goes out, he meets Arlo the cat or Popsie the dog.

My favourite animals are

....

9

Dragon Breath

Round the corner, not far away, Bing is feeling chilly today.

Bing is playing outside in the frosty garden. **Brrr!** – it's cold! And look – when he blows through his mouth, steam comes out!

"Hello Bing!" Pando crawls in through the gap in the fence.

Oh! Pando has got steam coming out of his mouth, too!

"Look Pando, I'm a dragon!" says Bing, blowing a large white cloud.

"I'm a train!" laughs Pando. "Choo choo!"

Bing runs inside. "Look Flop, I've got **dragon breath!**" He blows a big breath to show Flop.

But nothing comes out!

Flop smiles. He says dragon breath only works outside, where the air is **cold**. It's too **warm** in the kitchen.

"**Bi-ng!** Come and look at this!" shouts Pando.

Bing runs back outside. **Oh!** There's something icy on the garden tap. "What is it?" asks Pando. Bing snaps the icy thing off to show Flop.

"You've found an icicle," says Flop. "It's beautiful."

Brrr! The icicle is making Bing's hand feel icy cold.

"How about some hot chocolate to warm us up again?" asks Flop.

"Yup!"

Bing and Pando bring the icicle inside to play with, but Flop says icicles don't stay icy in the warm. So they put it in the freezer to keep cold while Flop makes hot chocolate.

"Don't drink it just yet, Bing," says Flop.

"We need to wait for it to cool down. It's still too hot."

Bing tries to wait, but waiting is hard! And his fingers are still cold from holding the icicle. So he dips them into his hot chocolate to warm them up!

Ouch!

"Oh dear, Bing Bunny, it was still too hot," says Flop. "Come on, let's get those fingers cooled down. Something cold will help take the hot away."

Poor Bing.

"I know!" says Pando. "What about the icicle?"

"Good idea, Pando!" Flop gets the icicle from the freezer. "Here, Bing."

The icicle **cools down** the hot in Bing's hand.

"Ah, it feels **better** now!"

"Good for you, Bing Bunny!" says Flop. "And good for you too, Pando!"

Pando and Bing want to drink their hot chocolate – but it's **still** too hot! "Let's put some ice in!" says Pando.

Flop fetches some **clean** ice cubes from the freezer. The ice cubes cool down the hot chocolate. Now it is **just right** for drinking!

Yum!

Hot and **cold**... it's a Bing thing!

Let's make inside icicles!

Icicles are made of icy water. They like being outside where the air is cold – if you bring them inside where it's warm, they'll melt away! Bing's making special inside icicles that won't melt – and you can too!

You will need:

- an apron
- old newspapers
- white paper
- tin foil
- paint in wintry colours – blue, white, silver, grey
- paper glue
- glitter – silver or blue
- a paintbrush
- sticky tape
- scissors
- wool or string

What to do:

1. Cover your table with old newspapers and put on an apron so you don't get too messy!

2. Now paint a few pieces of white paper in wintry colours – try breezy blue and chilly grey! When you've finished, leave your paper to dry.

3. While you're waiting, take a square of tin foil and roll it up from one corner into a cone shape. Squish and squash it so the foil crinkles and looks more glittery. Make as many tin foil icicles as you like.

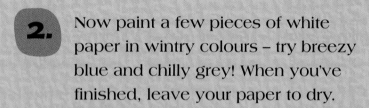

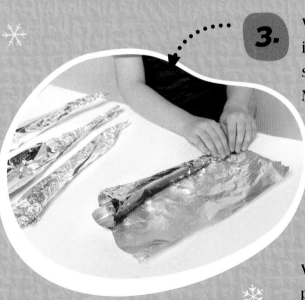

4.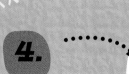

When your painted paper is dry, cut it into icicle-shaped triangles.

5. If you want to make your icicles extra-frosty and glittery, dot some glue on to the paper and sprinkle glitter on top.

6. Fold the wide end of a paper icicle over the string and stick it down with tape.

7. Next, fix a tin foil icicle on to the string and then another paper one – mix them up however you want!

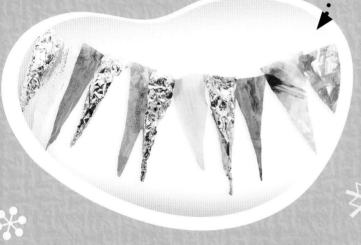

8. Good for you! Beautiful, glittery icicles that won't melt when they're inside! Where will you hang them?

Brrr!

Time to go back indoors to make some inside icicles!

Hot and cold, rain or shine

There are **cold** days and there are **hot** days, but there are lots of **other** kinds of days, too! The weather changes **all the time!**

Sunny weather

When the **sun** is out, the air feels warm. Sometimes it can be **too** warm and you have to sit down in the shade to **cool** down again. On **really** sunny days, Bing gets an ice cream from Gilly's van – that keeps him **cool**.

Rainy weather

On a **wet weather** day, the sky is **full** of clouds. The clouds get bigger and **bigger**, darker and **darker**, until – **splish!** – they drop water everywhere. After the rain has stopped, Bing and Sula go jumping in the puddles.
Splish! Splash! Splosh!

How do y...
Hot
Warm
Coo...

Windy weather

Windy days feel **whooshy** on your face. The leaves **rustle** in the trees and umbrellas turn **inside out!** When it's **windy**, Bing goes to the park to play with his Hoppity Voosh kite. He runs **really** fast and then – whooosh! – the kite flies up, up, **up** into the air!

Snowy weather

Sometimes in the winter, the clouds get so cold that they freeze the rain into snow. The snowflakes **float** down out of the sky, and fall on the **ground**, making everything **snowy** and **white!**

Rainbows

Sometimes, there can be rain and sunshine at the same time, and a colourful **rainbow** will appear in the sky. Have you ever seen one? Rainbows don't stay around for very long, but they are **very** pretty.

Angry clouds

Bing loves **laughing** and **playing** with his friends
– Sula, Pando, Coco... and Charlie, too!

But **sometimes,** Bing and his friends **don't** have fun when they play together. Instead, they make each other feel **angry.**

Here are some things that make Bing cross and upset.
Do these things make **you** feel angry, **too**?

How do you feel when...

...you want a turn – now!

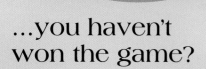

...you haven't won the game?

...someone won't share?

...your special toy gets broken?

...you want to be in charge?

...someone shouts?

When **you** feel angry, try taking a **deep breath...** then **blow away** your angry into a cloud

— *pfffffffff!*

That's it! There goes all that angry.

Bye, bye, angry cloud!

Bing things for a rainy day

Some days, when it's **cold** and **wet** outdoors, Bing likes to play inside. Here are some Bing things for you to try on **rainy days.**

Found you, Bing!

Hide and seek

Where are **your** best places to hide?

Make a cake

Bing likes **decorating** his cakes with **fruit.** What will you use?

Toy tea party

Bing has brought **Hoppity Voosh.** Who will you invite to **your** party?

Build a house

Sofa cushions, blankets and pillows all make **great** walls!

Sticky pictures

Bing's using **feathers** and **pasta** in his picture for Sula. You could use leaves or flowers, pictures from magazines, sweet wrappers... **what else?**

There – all done!

Cleaning up!

Oops – Bing's done a clumbo! If you make a mess, it's no big thing – help clean it up again!

Voo Voooo...

Rainy days can be the **busiest, best** days of **all!**

My year with Bing

Spring, summer, autumn, winter...
it's been a **busy year!**
Here are some of Bing's **best** days,
and **my** best ones, too.

Putting on a show in the park

Learning to skateboard

Getting a yummy delicious
carroty ice cream from Gilly

Collecting acorns with Sula

Watching fireworks
go **bang** in the sky

Nature Explorer

Round the corner,
not far away,
Bing and his friends
are exploring today.

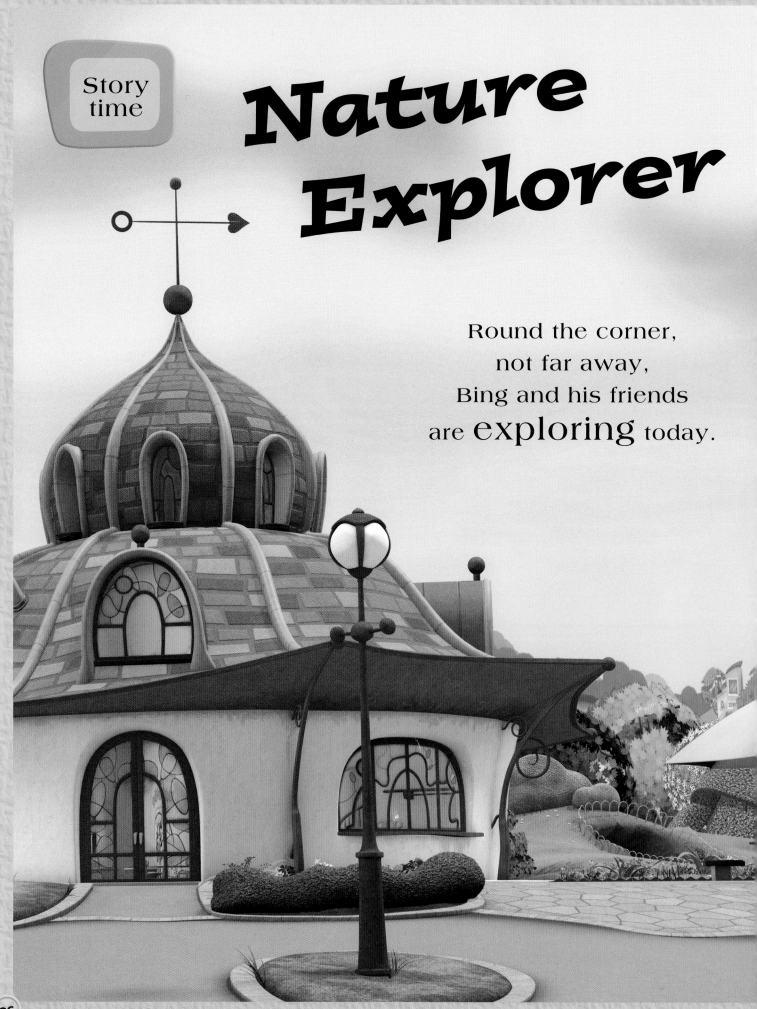

It's **circle time** at the crèche. Today Amma has something special to show everyone.

"A rainy-bow!" shouts Bing.

"Yes, Bing," smiles Amma. "It's a colour wheel – with all the **colours** of the rainbow! Now... who's ready to be a **Nature Explorer?**"

"Oh!"   "Me!"
     "I am!"

Sula goes first. She spins the colour wheel. It goes

tuk-tuk-tuk-tuk-tuk...

– fast at first, and then slower and slower – until it stops on... yellow!

"Now Sula," says Amma. "Look carefully around you, and try to find something **yellow.**" Sula looks around.

There! She spots a yellow dandelion.

It's Coco's turn next.

tuk-tuk-tuk-tuk-tuk...

Red! Coco finds her favourite red thing of all. "A ladybird!"

tuk-tuk-tuk-tuk-tuk...

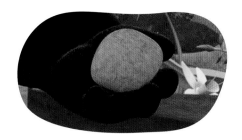

Pando finds an **orange pebble.** Well done, Pando!

Now it's Bing's turn.

tuk-tuk-tuk-tuk-tuk...

Purple! Hmm... Bing runs over to a purple flower. "Careful, Bing," warns Flop. "Explorers have to **look closely.**"

Bing looks at the flower.
Oh! It's a **thistle** – with pointy prickles.

Bing wants to take the thistle to Amma,
but the prickles are **sharp.**

"How about this?" says Flop. He gives
Bing his phone. Bing takes a **photo**
of the thistle. **There!**

"Good for you, Bing Bunny!"
smiles Amma. "Now, who's next?"

The Nature Explorers have lots of
goes with the colour wheel.
Sula points to the **blue** sky.

Coco finds a **red** leaf, then Pando
finds **another red** leaf.

"One more spin, then it's time
for lunch," says Amma.

It's Bing's turn again. He's going to
be the **last** Nature Explorer!

tuk-tuk-tuk-tuk-tuk...

Oh! Red – again!

Like Coco and Pando, Bing can see lots more red leaves... but he wants to find something new.

Then – "Look!" he shouts. "I've found something red!" It's a raspberry. Bing reaches out to pick it, but –

ouch!

– he touches a pointy prickle

"Ow ow ow!"

Poor Bing. His finger is very sore.

"What happened, Bing?" asks Flop.

"I wanted to get a red raspberry," sobs Bing. "But it **prickled** my finger."

"**Poor** bunny," says Amma. She puts a plaster on Bing's finger to help make it better again.

Bing still needs something red. Flop has an idea.

He finds a stick and pulls the prickles out of the way.

Carefully, Bing reaches to get the raspberry. "**I picked** it Flop!"

"Indeed," smiles Flop. "**Good for you, Bing Bunny!**"

Being a Nature Explorer... it's a **Bing thing.**

Hunting for colours

Bing and his friends are great Nature Explorers. Would YOU like to be one, too?

Things in nature are all different colours. Can YOU find something for every colour on these pages – in the garden, in the park, or even at home?

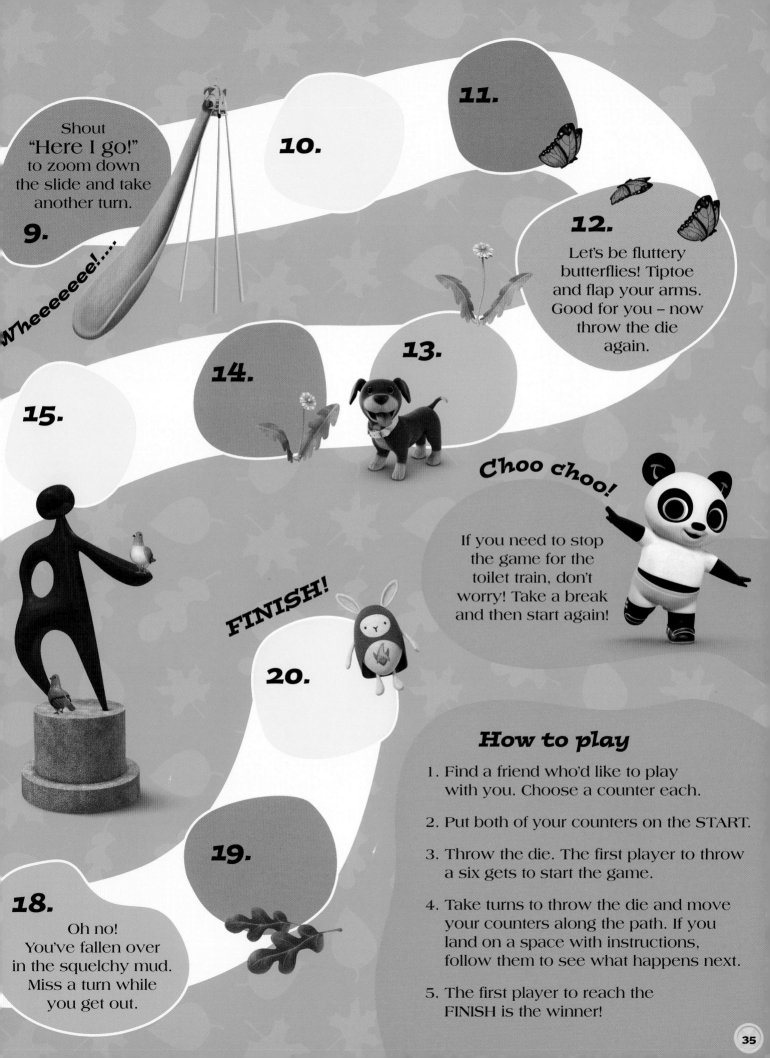

Shout "Here I go!" to zoom down the slide and take another turn.

9.

Wheeeeeee!...

10.

11.

12.

Let's be fluttery butterflies! Tiptoe and flap your arms. Good for you – now throw the die again.

13.

14.

15.

Choo choo!

If you need to stop the game for the toilet train, don't worry! Take a break and then start again!

FINISH!

20.

19.

18.

Oh no! You've fallen over in the squelchy mud. Miss a turn while you get out.

How to play

1. Find a friend who'd like to play with you. Choose a counter each.

2. Put both of your counters on the START.

3. Throw the die. The first player to throw a six gets to start the game.

4. Take turns to throw the die and move your counters along the path. If you land on a space with instructions, follow them to see what happens next.

5. The first player to reach the FINISH is the winner!

Ask a grown-up to help set up your paints.

Let's make painty butterflies!

You will need:

- an apron
- old newspapers
- several sheets of white A4 paper
- a paintbrush
- splodgy paints in lots of different colours

You could also use:

- crayons, pens or pencils
- paper glue
- glitter
- a straw

Butterflies can be lots of different colours. Bing's going to make butterfly pictures using all his favourite colours! Can you make some too?

What to do:

1. Put on an apron and spread old newspapers over the table to keep it clean.

2. Take a piece of paper and fold it in half. Then open it out flat again.

4. Next, fold the white half of the paper on top of the painty half and press it together. Can you feel the paint squishing inside as you wipe your hands over the paper?

3. Use your brush to splodge some paint on one half of your paper. Make sure you leave the other half of the paper white.

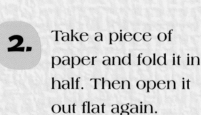

5. Carefully peel apart the paper and... ta-daa! A beautiful painty butterfly! You can make lots more butterflies – and each one will be different!

Ta-daa!

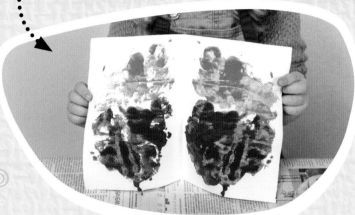

6. Use some pinchy pegs to hang all your butterflies up to dry. If you leave them outside they'll flutter in the breeze!

7. If you want to, when your butterfly is dry, put some glue on the wings and then sprinkle sparkly glitter on top. You could use your pens and crayons to decorate its wings with pretty patterns and shapes.

8. If you add water to your paint to make it really runny, you can blow through a straw to make new shapes before you fold your paper in half.

What lovely, fluttery, painty butterflies!

At Padget's shop

Bing and Sula are helping Flop with the **shopping**. They are looking for a **pineapple**, but Padget can't remember where she **put it!**

Can you help them to find it?

Now see if you can find these things hiding on the shelves.

carton of milk

cleaning spray

carrot torch

cereal

Flop needs 5 oranges. Do you think there are enough?

Good for you!

Choose a **lollipop** for helping. Which **colour** would you like?

cheese grater

carrot muffin

Me and Bing...
and all of our friends!

Bing **loves** playing with his friends.

This is **Charlie**. He loves playing with Bing's blocks – especially the red one!

Coco likes **dressing up** and dancing – and showing everyone what to do!

I love playing with **my** friends, too.

.... is my

funniest friend.

They make me **laugh**

because ....

....

....

Here comes Pando –
woohoo!
He likes running
around and
climbing things.

Sula **loves**
to do sparkle magic.
She is Bing's
best friend.

My **noisiest** friend is

My **best** friend is

....

....

Our favourite game is

We're best friends because

....

....

Surprise Machine

Round the corner, not far away,

Bing and Sula are **shopping** today.

Bing, Flop and Sula are at Padget's shop.
They have a list of **things to buy**.

"Good morning everyone," says Padget.
"What a long list!"

"Indeed," smiles Flop. **"Ready, you two?"**

But Bing and Sula have spotted something new.
"What is it, Padget?" asks Bing.

"It's my new **surprise machine**," says Padget.
"First you put a coin in. Then, you turn the
handle... the toy tumbles down...

...and out pops a **surprise!**"

Bing looks at all the
toys you can get.

"I'm going to get the **orange**
one," says Bing.

"Well, you **might** get
the orange one," says Flop,
"...or you might get a
different one instead."

Padget nods. "If you always
get the toy you want, there's
no surprise!"

Bing and Sula ask if they can put a coin into the
surprise machine.

"Sure," says Flop. "But let's do our shopping first."

"Come on, Bing!" says Sula.

"Let's do **super-quick shopping!**"

Once they've found everything on their list, Flop gives a coin to Sula, and one to Bing.

"Thank you, Flop."

Sula puts her coin into the surprise machine.
She turns the handle. She **really** wants the silver toy.

Ping!

A ball comes rolling down the chute.

"What is it?" asks Bing. Sula opens the ball.

The silver rhino! Lucky Sula
– she got what she wanted!

Now it's Bing's turn.
He puts his coin into
the surprise machine.
He turns the handle.
He really,

really,

really

wants the

orange toy.

Ping!

Bing's surprise rolls down the chute.

"What did you get?"
asks Sula.

Bing opens the ball. Oh! Bing got the green toy.
That's not the surprise he wanted.

Sula is spinning her silver toy round and round on the counter. Bing tries to spin his green toy, but it **doesn't work.**

"Oh... I don't **want** this one," sighs Bing.

Bing feels sad. He lets his toy roll onto the floor.

"**Look!**" shouts Bing. "It bounces!"

"Oh – I didn't know it did that!" gasps Sula. "And it's got **googly eyes!**"

Boiiinnnng!

"Oh, that is a surprise!" says Padget.

"Indeed," smiles Flop.

Surprises... sometimes, they're a Bing thing!

To the shop with Bing and Flop!

Flop and Bing are going to Padget's shop. But they're not in a hurry and there are lots of interesting things to see on the way.

Meow!

Pando's house

Meow!

Hello Bing, I have a letter here for Sula.

Let's follow Mitten.

Hello Arlo! Where are you going?

Come on Bing – off we go to the shop!

Let's take Sula her letter!

Bing's house

Oh! Look at Mitten's kittens.

Who wants a carroty muffin from from Padget's shop?

Playground

Shall we go and play on the slide?

Wak! Wak!

Duck pond

Sula's house

Oh look, acorns!

Woods

Cheeky Mr Squirrel!

Let's make a picnic lunch

Picnics are **great** – you can pack them up and take them with you anywhere! Just roll out a blanket in the **park** or in the **garden**, like Bing and his friends. And don't worry if it's raining – you can have a picnic **indoors**, too! Let's start by making our **sandwiches**.

Sandwiches

1. First choose the kind of bread you'd like.

2. Now pick your fillings. Mmm! What will you have?

white bread

brown bread

pitta bread

bagel

bread roll

tortilla

cheese

houmous

ham

tuna

chicken

avocado

carrot

egg

cucumber

lettuce

tomato

Almost there! What shape do you want your sandwich to be?

My fravrit sandwich is carroty bagel moons!

Mine's tomato pitta fingers!

squares

triangles

pockets

moons

I like cheesy brown bread triangles the best!

fingers

4. Finished? Good for you! Now draw a picture of your sandwich in the space below.

wraps

My favourite sandwich is...

Yummy delicious!

Sandwiches are just **part** of a picnic. There are **lots** more things that you can add: sticks and dips, **rainybow** fruit or yummy drinks... they're all a Bing thing!

Mmm!

Pick and dip

Do you like **picky, dippy** picnics? Sula does! Lay out bread sticks, cucumber, peppers and celery all together on a plate. **Mix up** some of Bing's favourite carroty spread (just cream cheese and grated carrot) and put it in a bowl. Now **pick**... and **dip**!

Yummy!

Rainybow fruit

Look at all these colours! Pick out some **fresh fruit** in lots of different colours, then lay everything out on a plate like a **rainybow.** You could try:

Purple
- blackberries
- grapes

Green
- grapes
- kiwi

Yellow
- pineapple
- banana
- melon

Red
- strawberries
- raspberries
- cherries

Blue
- blueberries of course!

Orange
- satsumas
- oranges
- mango

Smoothies

Our picnic is **nearly** ready, but we've forgotten one important thing... **drinks!** Bing likes smoothies best.

Good for you, Bing Bunny!

If you want to make a yummy smoothie, you have to put some fruit in Brenda the Blender. Then you put in some milk, press the button and *go, go, go, go, go!*

Try making up **your own** yummy delicious smoothie recipe. What will you use?

Raspberry mooshies

If you want a really **co-o-old** drink, raspberry mooshies are the **best!** Put ice cubes, raspberries and apple juice into your blender, press the button and *go, go, go, go, go* again!

Be careful with scissors. Ask a grown-up to help you.

Let's make eggy heads!

You will need:

- an empty eggshell
- an egg cup or egg box
- stick-on googly eyes
- cotton wool
- cress seeds
- water
- scissors
- felt-tip pens

Amma is showing Bing how to make eggy heads. They have oval faces, googly eyes and if you can wait long enough... green spiky hair! You can make one, too.

What to do:

1. Take an empty eggshell and sit it in an egg cup or egg box carton.

2. Now your eggy head needs a face! Be very careful not to break the shell. Start by sticking on some googly eyes. Next use your felt-tips to give your eggy a nose, mouth, eyelashes... whatever you like!

3. Make a little ball out of cotton wool, and dip it in some water.

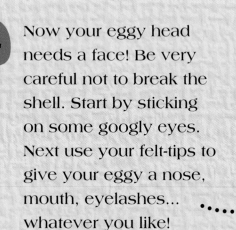

4. When the cotton wool is nice and wet, put it gently into your eggy head.

5. Now for the hair! Sprinkle some cress seeds on to the cotton wool.

Make sure that you put plenty on so there is a nice, even layer, but not too many or they won't grow!

7. Now you have to wait. This bit can be hard! Make sure you give your eggy a few drops of water now and then to stop the seeds from drying out.

6. Your eggy head needs light to help it grow hair. Put it in a sunny spot – a windowsill is perfect.

8. After a few days – woo-hoo! – your eggy head should have green cress hair! Now you can give your eggy a haircut. You can eat the cress hair too – what does it taste like?

Woo-hoo!

TIP:
Eggy hair is delicious with a hard-boiled egg and a little bit of mayonnaise.

"Mine's called Sula, because she looks just like me!"

"Mine's called Eggy!"

"Mine's Monster. Grrr!"

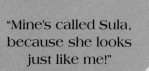

"This one is Shelly!"

Have you given your eggy head a name?

Bing's favourite things...

Hoppity Voosh is Bing's **favourite** toy.

Mmmm... yummy delicious!

Bing's favourite food is **crunchy carrots.**

and mine too!

My favourite toy is

....

My favourite food is

....

Bing's favourite **colour** is orange, because it's the colour of **carrots!**

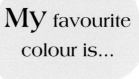
My favourite colour is...

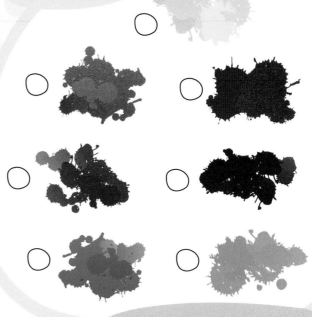

because

....

....

Bing's favourite story is all about... guess who?

Yup – **Hoppity Voosh!**

It's called

Hoppity Voosh and the Lonely Lettuce.

My favourite story is called

....

....

....

Bedtime storymaker

Bing is ready for bed.

Bath done?
Yup!

Jamas on?
Yup!

Teeth brushed?
Yup!

There's just one thing left to do...
a **story!**

Let's **make up** a Hoppity Voosh story **together.** Look at the words and follow the story. Every time you see this ✦, **you** choose what happens next.

Hoppity Voosh was snoozing...

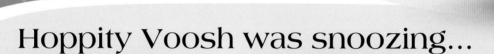

- ✦ in his hammock
- ✦ on the moon
- ✦ in a treehouse
- ✦ (somewhere else?)

when he heard...

- ✦ a bangy noise.
- ✦ a shouty scream.
- ✦ a sniffly sound.
- ✦ (another noise?)

Hoppity Voosh jumped up. "What's that?" he cried.

Oh! The sound was coming from a Star. The Star was...

- ✦ sad.
- ✦ cross.
- ✦ lonely.
- ✦ (what do you think?)

The Star was afraid of the dark.
Poor Star!

Hoppity Voosh wanted to help the Star.
So he vooshed to the rescue and...

- ✦ switched on the sky to take the dark away.

- ✦ sang a song to cheer the Star up.

- ✦ invited the Star to a tea party on the moon.

- ✦ (or something else?)

Voooooooooosh!

And the Star was happy again.
"Thank you, Hoppity Voosh!" said the Star.

Hoppity waved goodbye and
vooshed all the way back home,
just in time for a yummy delicious tea of...

- ✦ moon muffins.
- ✦ rocket bagels.
- ✦ space spaghetti.
- ✦ (what else is yummy delicious?)

The End

Telling
bedtime
stories... it's
a Bing thing.

Time to sleep now, Bing.

Goodnight, Hoppity!